THE OYSTER MUSHROOM PRODUCTION HANDBOOK

STEP-BY-STEP GUIDE ON OYSTER MUSHROOM PRODUCTION

OLANIRAN TAJUDEEN

DEDICATION

THIS BOOK IS DEDICATED TO MY LATE PARENT, MR. AND MRS. OLANIRAN, AND MY DAUGHTER, OLANIRAN AISHA ENIOLA.

CONTENTS

INTRODUCTION:

The oyster mushroom (scientific name: Pleurotus ostreatus) is a type of edible mushroom that is widely cultivated and consumed. It has a unique appearance with a fan-like or oyster-shaped cap, hence the name "oyster" mushroom. Let's explore the biological characteristics and life cycle of this fascinating fungus.

The oyster mushroom is a saprophytic organism, which means that it obtains its nutrients from decomposing organic matter, such as dead wood or plant debris. It plays an essential role in the decomposition and recycling of organic material in forest ecosystems.

The life cycle of the oyster mushroom starts with spore germination. The spores are tiny, reproductive cells that can be released from the gills of mature mushrooms. When conditions are suitable, spores land on a suitable substrate and germinate, forming thread-like structures called hyphae.

As the hyphae grow, they undergo a process called mycelium formation. Mycelium refers to a network of interconnected hyphae, which is the vegetative body of the mushroom. The mycelium spreads and colonizes the substrate, breaking down complex organic compounds into simpler forms that the mushroom can absorb and utilize for growth.

Once the mycelium has colonized the substrate, it undergoes a process called "primordia formation." Primordia are tiny, pin-like structures that develop on the substrate's surface. These primordia eventually grow and differentiate into mature mushrooms.

The oyster mushroom's fruiting body, which is the visible part of the mushroom we recognize, consists of a stem and a cap. The stem is cylindrical and centrally attached to the cap. The cap is oyster-shaped, ranging in color from pale gray to dark brown, with gills on the underside. These gills contain the mushroom's spores,which are dispersed into the environment for reproduction.

Under suitable conditions of moisture, temperature, and light, the primordial develop and elongate, forming mature mushrooms. The cap expands and flattens out, while the gills become more distinct.The mushrooms continue to grow until they reach maturity, at which point they can be harvested for consumption.

It's important to note that environmental conditions, such as temperature, humidity, and light, greatly influence the growth and development of oyster mushrooms. Therefore, careful control of these factors is required in commercial cultivation to ensure optimal mushroom production.

In conclusion, the oyster mushroom has a fascinating life cycle that starts with spore germination, followed by mycelium formation, and primordial development,and ultimately culminates in the growth of mature mushrooms. Understanding these biological and life cycle aspects is essential for the successful cultivation and harvesting of this delicious.

Certainly! The oyster mushroom is not only delicious but also offers several nutritional benefits. Here are some key nutritional values of oyster mushrooms per 100 grams:

Calories: Approximately 33 calories

Carbohydrates: Around 7 grams

Protein: Approximately 3.3 grams

Fat: Less than 0.5 grams

Fiber: Around 1 gram

Vitamins: Oyster mushrooms are a good source of various vitamins, including B vitamins such as niacin, riboflavin, and pantothenic acid.

Minerals: They provide essential minerals such as potassium, phosphorus, and copper.

Oyster mushrooms are highly versatile in the culinary world and can be used in a variety of dishes. Here are some popular culinary uses:

Sauteed or Stir-fried: Oyster mushrooms have a delicate flavor and tender texture, making them ideal for sauteing or stir-frying. They can be paired with vegetables, meats, or tofu to create flavorful and nutritious dishes.

Soups and Stews: Oyster mushrooms add depth and earthy flavors to soups and stews. They can be sliced or diced and added to various recipes like mushroom soup, vegetable broth, or hearty stews for added taste and texture.

Grilled or Roasted: Oyster mushrooms can be grilled or roasted to create a delicious and meaty texture. Marinating them before grilling or roasting can enhance their flavor and provide a satisfying alternative for vegetarians and vegans.

Asian Cuisine: Oyster mushrooms are widely used in Asian cuisine, particularly in dishes like mushroom stir-fries, hot pots, and noodle dishes. Their subtle flavor works well with traditional Asian seasonings and sauces.

Vegan Meat Substitutes: Due to their meaty texture, oyster mushrooms can be used as a plant-based substitute for meat. They can be used in dishes like mushroom burgers, mushroom tacos, or mushroom "pulled pork" sandwiches.

It's important to note that oyster mushrooms should be properly cooked before consumption to enhance their taste and ensure safety. Additionally, always ensure that you source oyster mushrooms from reliable and reputable sources.

DIFFERENT VARIETIES OF OYSTER MUSHROOMS

Oyster mushrooms come in various varieties, each with unique characteristics in terms of flavor, texture, and appearance. While the most commodity-cultivated variety is Pleurotus Ostreatus, several other lesser-known species offer exciting flavors and textures. Let's explore some of the different varieties of oyster mushrooms.

1.   **PLEUROTUS OSTREATUS**: Also known as the pearl oyster mushroom or grey oyster mushroom, Pleurotus ostreatus is the most widely cultivated variety of oyster mushrooms. It has a mild flavor and a delicate texture that becomes velvety when cooked. The caps are usually grayish-white or grayish-brown in color.

2.   **PLEUROTUS PULMONARIUS**: Commonly known as the phoenix oyster mushroom or lung oyster mushroom. Pleurotus pulmonarius is similar to Pleurotus ostreatus but with a slightly stronger flavor profile. It has a creamy white cap with a wavy margin and can grow larger than Pleurotus ostreatus.

3.   **PLEUROTUS ERYNGII**: Also called king oyster mushroom or trumpet royale, Pleurotus eryngii has a district cylindrical shape with a thick stem and small cap. It has a meaty texture and rich umami flavor that resembles seafood or shellfish. This variety is often used in Asian cuisine for stir-fries or grilling.

4.   **PLEUROTUS CITRINOPILEATUS**:   Known as the golden oyster mushroom, Pleurotus citrinopileatus has a vibrant yellow or change color that adds visual appeal to dishes. It has a mild and

slightly fruity flavor with a delicate texture. This variety is often used in salads or as a garnish.

5.   **PLEUROTUS CORNUCOPIAE**: Also called the branched oyster mushroom or abalone mushroom, Pleurotus cornucopia has a unique appearance with multiple caps growing from a single stem. It has a firm texture and a rich, earthy flavor. This variety is often used in soups or sauteed dishes.

These are just a few examples of the different varieties of oyster mushrooms available. Each variety offers its district taste and texture, allowing for endless culinary possibilities.

MUSHROOM CULTIVATION PROCESS

Mushroom cultivation involves creating the ideal conditions for the growth and development of mushrooms. The process typically involves the following steps:

Strain Selection: Choose a suitable strain of mushroom for cultivation. Oyster mushrooms, for example, have different strains with varied characteristics and growth requirements.

Substrate Preparation: Prepare the substrate, which serves as the growing medium for the mushrooms. Common substrates for oyster mushrooms include straw, sawdust, or a combination of both. The substrate is usually pasteurized or sterilized to eliminate competing organisms and create a favorable environment for the mushroom mycelium to grow.

Inoculation: Inoculate the substrate with mushroom spawn. Spawn is the mycelium from a selected strain of mushrooms that serves as the source of fungal growth. It is typically mixed with the prepared substrate, either through layering or mixing, to introduce the mushroom mycelium.

Incubation: Place the inoculated substrate in a controlled environment, typically in a dark and humid room with optimal temperature conditions. During this stage, the mycelium begins to colonize the substrate, spreading and establishing itself throughout the growing medium.

Casing Layer (optional): For certain mushroom varieties like oyster mushrooms, a layer of casing material can be spread over the colonized substrate. The casing layer provides additional favorable conditions for fruiting and helps to maintain humidity levels.

Fruiting: Once the mycelium has fully colonized the substrate or casing layer, environmental conditions are adjusted to stimulate fruiting. This includes providing the right combination of temperature, humidity, and light. Oyster mushrooms, for example, prefer cooler temperatures (around 18-24°C) and high humidity levels (around 85-95%).

Harvesting: As the mushrooms mature, they are harvested by gently twisting and pulling them from the substrate. It's crucial to harvest them at the right stage of maturity to ensure optimal flavor and texture.

Post-Harvest Care: After harvesting, the substrate can be composted or reused for subsequent mushroom cultivation cycles. Proper cleaning and sanitization of the growing area are necessary before starting a new cultivation cycle.

It's important to note that different mushroom varieties may have specific requirements and cultivation techniques. Therefore, it's essential to follow specific guidelines and consult reliable sources or experts for detailed instructions on cultivating the specific mushroom variety you are interested in.

OPTIMAL CONDITIONS FOR MYCELIUM GROWTH

Mycelium growth is a critical stage in the cultivation of fungi, whether for culinary, medicinal, or industrial purposes. The optimal conditions for mycelium growth can vary depending on the specific type of fungus you are cultivating. However, there are some general factors to consider:

Substrate: The substrate is the material on which the mycelium grows. Different fungi have different substrate preferences. Common substrates include grain (like rice or wheat), sawdust, wood chips, or a mixture of these.

Temperature: Temperature plays a crucial role in mycelium growth. Different fungi have different temperature preferences, but a range between 75-80°F (24-27°C) is suitable for many species. It's essential to maintain a consistent temperature throughout the mycelial growth phase.

Humidity: Fungi generally thrive in high-humidity environments. Humidity levels around 90-95% are often recommended during the mycelium growth stage. This can be achieved by misting the growing environment or using a humidification system.

Ventilation: Adequate air exchange is necessary to provide oxygen for mycelial growth and to remove carbon dioxide. Fungi need oxygen to respire and grow efficiently. While airtight conditions are suitable for some stages of cultivation, mycelium growth benefits from a well-ventilated environment.

pH Levels: The pH of the substrate can influence mycelium growth. Most fungi prefer slightly acidic to neutral conditions. A pH range between 5.5 and 7 is generally suitable for many fungi.

Light: Unlike plants, fungi don't photosynthesize, so they don't require light for energy production. However, some studies suggest that light can influence the direction of mycelial growth, and a light-dark cycle may be beneficial for certain fungi.

Sterility: Maintaining a sterile environment is crucial to prevent contamination by unwanted microorganisms. Use proper sterilization techniques for your equipment, substrate, and workspace.

Inoculation: Ensure that the inoculation process is done under sterile conditions to introduce the fungal spores or mycelium culture to the substrate without contamination.

Agitation: Some fungi benefit from regular, gentle agitation during the mycelium growth phase. This helps distribute nutrients, improve oxygenation, and encourage uniform growth.

Remember that these are general guidelines, and the optimal conditions can vary for different fungi. Always refer to specific cultivation guides or research for the particular species you are working with.

HARVESTING TECHNIQUES FOR MAXIMUM YIELD AND QUALITY.

Harvesting mushrooms involves careful timing and proper techniques to ensure maximum yield and quality. The specific methods can vary depending on the type of mushroom you are cultivating, but here are some general harvesting techniques that can help optimize yield and quality:

1. **Harvesting Timing:**

Harvest mushrooms when the caps are fully expanded but before they start to flatten out or turn upward. This is the stage when the mushrooms are most tender and flavorful.

Harvest before the veil (a thin membrane beneath the cap) breaks. Once the veil breaks, spore release begins, and the quality of the mushroom may decline.

2. **Cleanliness and Sterility:**

Maintain cleanliness during harvesting to minimize the risk of contamination. Use clean, sanitized tools to cut or pluck mushrooms to avoid introducing contaminants.

3. **Cutting vs. Twisting:**

Depending on the type of mushroom, you may either cut the stem or gently twist and pull to harvest.

For some varieties, cutting with a clean knife just above the substrate is preferred to avoid damaging the mycelium.

4. Continuous Harvest:

Some mushroom species can produce multiple flushes. Harvest the mature mushrooms, and new ones will continue to emerge.

Harvesting in stages allows for a more extended harvesting period and potentially higher overall yield.

5. Frequency of Harvest:

Harvest mushrooms as soon as they reach maturity to encourage the development of new mushrooms.

Frequent and timely harvesting can promote a more extended and productive cropping cycle.

6. Post-Harvest Handling:

Handle harvested mushrooms with care to avoid bruising or damaging the delicate caps.

Place harvested mushrooms in a clean container, preferably one that allows for good air circulation.

7. Environmental Conditions:

Harvest during the cooler parts of the day to reduce moisture loss and maintain quality.

Ensure the harvesting environment is clean and well-ventilated to prevent contamination.

8. Storage:

If not consumed immediately, store harvested mushrooms in a cool, dark place or in the refrigerator to prolong shelf life.

Avoid storing mushrooms in plastic bags, as they can become slimy due to moisture retention.

9. Harvesting Tools:

Use appropriate tools, such as a sharp knife or scissors, to cut mushrooms cleanly without causing damage. Clean tools between each harvest to prevent the spread of contaminants.

Always refer to specific guidelines for the mushroom species you are cultivating, as different mushrooms may have unique requirements. Additionally, proper post-harvest care is crucial to maintaining the quality and freshness of the harvested mushrooms.

TROUBLESHOOTING AND COMMON ISSUES IN MUSHROOM PRODUCTION

Mushroom cultivation can be a rewarding but delicate process, and various issues can arise during different stages. Here are some common problems encountered in mushroom production and troubleshooting tips:

(I)   Contamination

Issue: Unwanted microorganisms competing with the mushroom mycelium.

Troubleshooting: Maintain a sterile environment, use proper sterilization techniques, and follow recommended hygiene practices. Ensure that all equipment and substrates are clean.

(II)   Slow or No Growth:

Issue: Mycelium not colonizing the substrate as expected.

Troubleshooting: Check and adjust environmental conditions, including temperature, humidity, and substrate quality. Ensure that the substrate is not too wet or dry. Verify the freshness of the spores or inoculum.

(III)   Abnormal Mushroom Growth:

Issue: Mushrooms with deformities, discoloration, or irregular shapes.

Troubleshooting: Inconsistent environmental conditions, poor substrate quality, or genetic issues may be the cause. Review and optimize growing

parameters and ensure the use of high-quality substrates.

(IV)   Poor Fruiting Body Formation:

Issue: Mushrooms not forming properly or failing to produce caps.

Troubleshooting: Check for adequate air exchange, humidity levels, and proper light conditions. Adjust the fruiting environment to promote proper fruiting body development.

(V)   Mushroom Diseases:

Issue: Fungal, bacterial, or viral infections affecting the crop.

Troubleshooting: Practice good hygiene, quarantine contaminated materials, and consider using disease-resistant strains. Adjust environmental conditions to discourage pathogen growth.

(VI)   Over-watering or Under-watering:

Issue: Incorrect moisture levels in the substrate.

Troubleshooting: Monitor and adjust watering practices. Ensure the substrate is consistently moist but not waterlogged. Use well-draining substrates and avoid over-watering.

(VII)   Inadequate Fruiting Conditions:

Issue: Failure to induce fruiting or poor fruiting conditions.

Troubleshooting: Adjust temperature, humidity, and light conditions according to the specific requirements of the mushroom species. Introduce fresh air regularly during the fruiting stage.

(VIII)   Insect Infestations:

Issue: Insects damaging mycelium or fruiting bodies.

Troubleshooting: Keep the cultivation area clean and free of organic debris. Use screens or nets to prevent insects from entering the growing area. Consider natural or chemical methods to control pests.

(IX)   Unusual Odors:

Issue: Foul or unpleasant smells in the cultivation area.

Troubleshooting: Check for contamination, especially bacterial contamination, and remove affected materials. Ensure proper air circulation and ventilation.

(X) Harvesting Issues:

Issue: Difficulty in harvesting or low yields.

Troubleshooting: Harvest mushrooms at the right stage, use clean and sharp tools, and follow proper harvesting techniques. Adjust environmental conditions to encourage continuous flushes.

Regular monitoring, attention to detail, and adherence to best practices in mushroom cultivation are essential for troubleshooting and preventing issues. Additionally, keeping detailed records can help identify patterns and potential sources of problems.

MARKETING STRATEGIES IN OYSTER MUSHROOM

Marketing is crucial for successfully selling oyster mushrooms or any other agricultural product. Here are some effective marketing strategies for oyster mushrooms:

1. Branding and Packaging:

Develop a distinctive brand for your oyster mushrooms. Create a memorable logo and design eye-catching packaging. Clear, attractive packaging can enhance product visibility and attract customers.

2. Local Farmers' Markets and Grocery Stores:

Participate in local farmers' markets or collaborate with nearby grocery stores. Build relationships with local retailers and consumers. Highlight the freshness and quality of your oyster mushrooms.

3. Online Presence:

Establish an online presence through a website or social media platforms. Showcase your oyster mushrooms, share cultivation stories, and engage with your audience. Consider selling directly to consumers through an online store.

4. Community Engagement:

Engage with the local community by attending events, sponsoring local activities, or collaborating with restaurants and chefs.

Create a positive image for your brand through community involvement.

5. Educational Content:

Share educational content about the nutritional benefits of oyster mushrooms, different culinary uses, and cultivation practices. This can be done through blog posts, social media, or workshops.

6. Collaborate with Restaurants and Chefs:

Approach local restaurants, chefs, and culinary influencers to feature your oyster mushrooms on their menus. Establishing partnerships with chefs can help create demand and increase your market reach.

7. CSA (Community Supported Agriculture) Programs:

Consider participating in or establishing a CSA program where consumers subscribe to regular deliveries of fresh oyster mushrooms. This provides a steady customer base and income.

8. Certifications and Quality Assurance:

Obtain relevant certifications, such as organic or sustainable certifications, to appeal to consumers who prioritize such qualities. Emphasize the quality and safety of your oyster mushrooms in your marketing efforts.

9. Customer Reviews and Testimonials:

Encourage satisfied customers to leave reviews and testimonials. Positive feedback can build credibility and attract new customers. Display these reviews on your website or marketing materials.

10. Seasonal Promotions:

Run seasonal promotions or discounts to attract customers during specific times of the year. Consider offering special packages or deals for bulk purchases.

11. Diversify Product Offerings:

Explore opportunities to diversify your product line, such as offering value-added products like mushroom powders, extracts, or ready-to-cook kits. This can expand your market and cater to different consumer preferences.

12. Networking with Other Farmers:

Network with other local farmers and businesses. Collaborate on joint marketing initiatives or share distribution channels to reach a broader audience.

13. Feedback and Improvement:

Actively seek customer feedback and use it to improve your products and marketing strategies. Respond to customer inquiries promptly and address any concerns to build trust.

Adapting your marketing strategies to the specific needs and preferences of your target market is key. Regularly evaluate and adjust your approach based on market trends, customer feedback, and the evolving demands of the industry.

CONCLUSION

Oyster mushroom production can be a rewarding venture, offering opportunities for sustainable agriculture and contributing to the growing demand for specialty mushrooms. In conclusion, a successful oyster mushroom production operation involves careful planning, precise cultivation techniques, and effective marketing strategies. Here are some key points to consider:

1. Cultivation Practices:

Establishing optimal conditions for mycelium growth and fruiting is crucial. This includes providing the right substrate, maintaining appropriate temperature and humidity levels, ensuring proper air exchange, and managing light conditions.

Attention to sterility during inoculation and substrate preparation helps prevent contamination and ensures a healthy mushroom crop.

Timely harvesting at the right stage of maturity is essential for maximizing yield and maintaining quality.

2. Troubleshooting and Problem Solving:

Regular monitoring of the cultivation environment allows for the early identification of issues such as contamination, slow growth, or abnormal fruiting. Troubleshooting and addressing problems promptly are critical to the success of the operation.

Implementing proper hygiene practices, adjusting environmental conditions, and using disease-resistant strains can help prevent and manage common issues.

3. Marketing Strategies:

Effective marketing is essential for reaching and expanding your customer base. Developing a strong brand, creating appealing packaging, and engaging with the local community through farmers' markets, grocery stores, and online platforms are key components.

Collaboration with chefs, restaurants, and other local businesses can increase visibility and demand for your oyster mushrooms.

4. Diversification and Innovation:

Exploring opportunities for diversification, such as offering value-added products or participating in Community Supported Agriculture (CSA) programs, can enhance the sustainability and profitability of your oyster mushroom production.

Staying informed about market trends, consumer preferences, and emerging technologies allows for innovation and adaptation to changing conditions.

5. Continuous Improvement:

Regularly seeking feedback from customers and incorporating improvements based on their suggestions contributes to customer satisfaction and loyalty.

Keeping abreast of advancements in cultivation techniques, sustainable practices, and marketing strategies helps your operation remain competitive.

6. Adaptability and Resilience:

Oyster mushroom production, like any agricultural endeavor, is subject to various external factors such as weather conditions, market fluctuations, and unforeseen challenges. Cultivating adaptability and resilience is crucial for navigating uncertainties and sustaining long-term success.

Successful oyster mushroom production requires a holistic approach that encompasses cultivation, marketing, and adaptability. By combining sound cultivation practices with effective marketing strategies and a commitment to continuous improvement, growers can establish a thriving and sustainable mushroom production operation.

This Oyster mushroom production handbook serves as a valuable resource for both novice and experienced cultivators. As you all know, oyster mushroom production is a sustainable and economically viable endeavor, offering a versatile culinary ingredient. Its fast growth, adaptability, and nutritional benefits make it a promising choice for small-scale or commercial cultivation.

It provides detailed insight into substrate selection, cultivation techniques, disease management, environmental conditions, and harvesting practices. The handbook's step-by-step guidance facilitates successful mushroom cultivation, contributing to increased yields and quality. Ongoing research and updates to the handbook can enhance its effectiveness, ensuring that it remains a reliable reference for individuals engaged in oyster mushroom production.

Finally, to help you scale up your operation or turn it into a profitable business venture, the handbook covers topics such as marketing strategies, packaging options, and distribution channels, which in turn increase sales and product awareness amongst competitors in the same business.

Printed in Great Britain
by Amazon

43410942R00020